MARVEL STUDIOS

THOR
LOVE AND THUNDER

"Eat my Hammer."

Rudely interrupted from his quest to find inner peace, Thor reunites with King Valkyrie, Korg, and Dr. Jane Foster – now The Mighty Thor – as they attempt to stop Gorr the God Butcher from killing all the gods.

TITAN EDITORIAL
Editor Jonathan Wilkins
Group Editor Jake Devine
Art Director Oz Browne
Editorial Assistant Ibraheem Kazi
Copy Editor Phoebe Hedges
Assistant Editor Calum Collins
Production Controller Kelly Fenlon
Production Controller Caterina Falqui
Production Manager Jackie Flook
Sales & Circulation Manager Steve Tothill
Marketing Coordinator Lauren Noding
Publicity & Sales Coordinator Alexandra Iciek
Publicity Manager Will O'Mullane
Digital & Marketing Manager Jo Teather
Head of Business & Creative Development
Duncan Baizley
Publishing Directors Ricky Claydon
& John Dziewiatkowski
Group Operations Director Alex Ruthen

Executive Vice President Andrew Sumner
Publishers Vivian Cheung & Nick Landau

DISTRIBUTION
U.S. Newsstand: Total Publisher Services, Inc.
John Dziewiatkowski, 630-851-7683
U.S. Newsstand Distribution: Curtis
Circulation Company

PRINTED IN CHINA

U.S. Bookstore Distribution: The News Group
U.S. Direct Sales: Diamond Comic Distributors

For more info on advertising contact adinfo@
titanemail.com

*Marvel Studios' Thor: Love and Thunder The Official
Movie Special* published September 2023 by Titan
Magazines, a division of Titan Publishing Group

Limited, 144 Southwark Street, London, SE1 0UP.
For sale in the U.S. and Canada.
ISBN: 9781787737235

Thanks to, Kevin Pearl, Samantha Keane, Rodney
Vallo, Shiho Tilley, and Eugene Paraszczuk at Disney.

Authorized User. No part of this publication may
be reproduced, stored in a retrival system, or
transmitted, in any form or by any means, without
the prior written permission of the publisher. A CIP
catalogue record for this title is available from the
British Library.

10 9 8 7 6 5 4 3 2 1

TITAN

MARVEL
© 2023 MARVEL

CONTENTS

CHRIS HEMSWORTH
THOR

Now bigger than ever, Chris Hemsworth returns as Thor to face his greatest adversary and reignite an old flame.

Where is Thor at the start of Marvel Studios' *Thor: Love and Thunder*?
At the end of Marvel Studios' *Avengers: Endgame*, we see a confused, lost version of Thor. He's certainly better at the end of the film than he was at the start of the film. But he still doesn't really know who he is or what his place is in the universe. He decides he needs to go out there and search and take some time for himself. And so travels off with the Guardians and much to their discomfort and irritation, he plants himself firmly in the center of their posse and tries to dictate how things should be run. He sees himself as the captain or the leader and that causes some friction within the group.

What was it like being back with the Guardians cast?
It was awesome. Some of the funnest stuff I had on the *Avengers* films·was interacting with them. It's just a very different pace with that group. There's a lot of improvisation, which is very much how we worked on Marvel Studios' *Thor: Ragnarok*. So that was a great opportunity to bounce back and forth from each other. I love working with every other Avenger. What's wonderful is everyone has a different energy. But with the Guardians there's a kind of a humor to it and a sort of irony and a wackiness that seems to fit mine and Taika's brain.

You and Chris Pratt seem to have a strong rapport.
He's just so funny and very generous when I'm acting opposite him. He's also hugely collaborative. You know, it's never about competing for jokes. It's basically about finding what's the funniest moment within the scene, and then you share the load. It doesn't really matter who gets to deliver the punchline. It's just about hitting the target in order to make the scene work.

01 Sparks fly as Chris Hemsworth takes up arms as Thor.

02 (Next Spread) Behind the scenes as Hemsworth joins the Guardians of the Galaxy.

▶

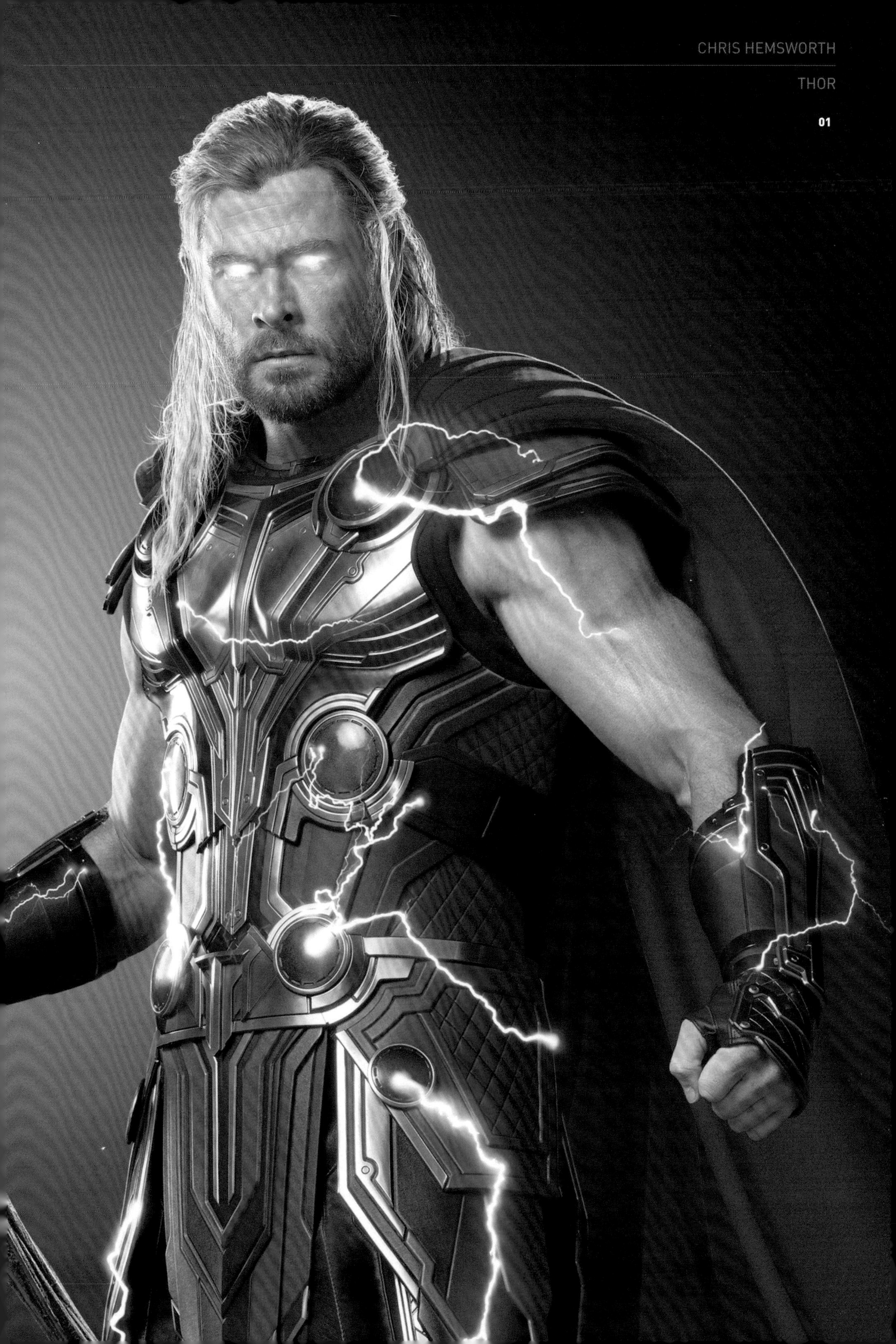

"Taika and I felt we really raised the bar with Marvel Studios' *Thor: Ragnarok* and that created a big expectation..."

► Was it good to be working with Taika again?
Marvel Studios' *Thor: Ragnarok* was obviously a huge change for us and really moved the needle into such a different territory from where we started. I remembered coming out of Marvel Studios' *Thor: Ragnarok* going into Marvel Studios' *Avengers: Infinity War* and Marvel Studios' *Avengers: Endgame*, and being adamant about trying to hang on to the new version of Thor and not go back to the old version. I made sure that everyone looked at what we'd shot on Marvel Studios' *Thor: Ragnarok* because that film hadn't come out yet. So the Russos got sent a few scenes so they could see the tone we were operating in. So then we were able to do something different again in Marvel Studios' *Avengers: Infinity War* and Marvel Studios' *Avengers: Endgame*.

There was a huge amount of pressure coming into Marvel Studios' *Thor: Love and Thunder*. Taika and I felt we really raised the bar with Marvel Studios'

Thor: Ragnarok and that created a big expectation for what we'd do next. It wasn't a case of dismantling it and reinventing it entirely again. It was a case of knowing that we were in the right zone from what we did in Marvel Studios' *Thor: Ragnarok* and to use the space and opportunity to expand on that. What really helped to build on the previous film was the new cast members and having Natalie Portman back. We have Christian Bale and Tessa Thompson. Adding new elements to it just pulled the story and the characters into different directions. There was heartbreak in Marvel Studios' *Thor: Ragnarok*. It was about loss and it was was about family struggles. It was about Thor trying to understand his place in the world, which is what he is trying to do in most of the films. Marvel Studios' *Thor: Love and Thunder* is a kind of romantic comedy. Taika had talked about that at one point and that set us on a certain path, which was going to be unique and different.

03 Thor and Stormbreaker bring on the thunder!

04 Chris Hemsworth and Taika Waititi mull over a scene on the set.

05 A behind the scenes shot as Thor arrives to defend New Asgard.

06 Thor swaps his enchanted weapon for a whisk as he swaps beating bad guys for ► beating eggs!

▶ How do you manage the balance between drama and comedy in each scene?"

You have to be true to that particular scene and that moment. Within that sort of space, you can't really think too much about it. You have to have a continuity with it, obviously. You've just got to react within that space. Whether that scene requires drama, heartache, love, or if it's just full comedy, it's got to be driving the story forward. You just have to service whatever it wants. I think we had a great script and foundation for that. We've gone from scenes that are so off the wall crazy that we wonder how are we going to get away with this kind of wackiness in something very real, rooted in drama. It certainly has a lot of ingredients, and makes the movie hard to pin it down as whether it is a comedy, a drama, or an action film.

The movie utilizes a new device called The Volume to create real locations for the actors to play against. Did you enjoy working with that technology?

It's been incredible. If you're standing on the edge of a cliff looking out into the sunset to actually be staring into a sunset certainly does pull out certain emotions and reactions from you that you may not get if it's your own imagination. It's very different staring at a blue or green screen. That's quite numbing and requires a whole lot more effort and imagination. Visually it's stunning because you get the actual reflection off the background of whatever it is you're looking at. In the scenes where there's beautiful sunsets there's a nice orange glow from the sun. If it's a scene where we're in outer space and there's all sorts of different colors and sparkles, then we're getting that as well. So there's, aesthetically, a beautiful interaction that occurs.

Do you prefer the long or short hair?

Short hair. I like that look with the semi-dreadlock hair and the beard and all that, especially in Marvel Studios' *Avengers: Endgame*, but that was the most uncomfortable look in the history of anything I've ever done. You've got glue on your face and on the beard, and then the wig is glued on. And there's pins and all sorts of other stuff. It's an extra hour or two in hair and makeup each day, so it's nice when we

07

08

09

07 Hemsworth dons a heroic pose in front of the camera.

08 An injured Sif warns Thor of Gorr's sinister intentions.

09 Behind the scenes on the bluescreen stage as Thor is brought in front of Zeus.

10 Thor is reunited with Mjölnir... or is he?

cut Thor's hair in the third film because I could just come in, put a bit of makeup on, and walk straight onto the set. Then, when we were doing the fourth film, we decided to give him long hair again!

Thor has some very unusal allies in the movie, namely the goats...
The goats were a gift from the king on the planet of Indigarr. They're manic and chaotic, but they're big, lovable creatures. So they come along for the ride. When, we need a vessel to transport us to different worlds, so we get this tourist ship from New Asgard and then we attach the goats to it. Then we put Stormbreaker on the front of it and off we go... even that description of our vehicle of choice kind of sums up the movie! ▶

▶ **What did you do to prepare physically for this movie?**
Each time I've played the character, I had to put the muscle and size on, and then lose it for another role playing another character. But you have muscle memory and it got easier each time. This was particularly hard I think because of the sort of target weight we aimed for was quite a ways above where I'd been before. This was probably the biggest I'd ever been, and I think the fittest. But we had twelve months where I was at home just training and exploring what I could do to get into the best shape. I tried swimming and Martial Arts, and tried different diets. It was a really fun exploration, and then I got really big and fit, but then I just had to hold it for four months, which was very hard.

Did you enjoy being reunited with Natalie Portman as Dr. Jane Foster?
Oh, it was so good. We had so much fun. I was just so happy. Natalie was hugely enthusiastic about doing another *Thor* movie. I think she'd seen Marvel Studios' *Thor: Ragnarok*, and she wanted to be in a film like that. She's up for anything, she's collaborative, fun, and has a great sense of humor. This is a very different direction for the character, and we had some real concerns about whether her character matches what we had seen before and had continuity. It was like what happened in Marvel Studios' *Thor: Ragnarok*. We went for a kind of a rebirth or a new exploration of the character. Natalie was completely down for it. It's worked out so well. It's been so much fun to work with her again.

11 Thor captured in Ominipotence City, home of Zeus.

12 Thor and The Mighty Thor.

13 Thor shows off his great strength.

14 Thor brandishes Zeus' Thunderbolt.

15 Gorr strikes down as Thor defends himself with Zeus' Thunderbolt.

16 Dr. Jane Foster is reunited with Thor.

"This was probably the biggest I've ever been."

Why is Christian Bale such an effective presence as Gorr the God Butcher?

Oh man, he's just so talented. I've been so lucky to work with so many brilliant performers. And then, every now and again, you work with someone so good, it's like a slap in the face. And even in a setting like this where you're still doing everything you can to make it real and truthful. But there's so much drama and insanity around it, it sometimes just gets lost within the chaos. But Christian manages just to pull the focus right into that moment. You can't take your eyes off him. The character is fascinating because like all good villains, he actually has a point. He may not be going about it the right way, but a good villainous character manages to pull some empathy or manipulate you into thinking they might be right. It has a lot to do with the script, but Christian brought so much to the character. He added more layers and depth to Gorr which then just made me think even harder about what Thor's point of view is. Their relationship is not as simple as Thor coming in to save the day from the villain. It was a lot more complex than that. We have some really beautiful scenes with him.

▶ Thor is also reunited with Valkyrie. Did you enjoy working with Tessa Thompson again?

It was fantastic—I love working with Tessa. I've done several films with her in this world and outside of it. When we meet her again, she's the King of New Asgard but its basically an administrative kind of role. She's signing documents and cutting the ribbons to openings of stores and things, which is not where she wants to be. She's a warrior at heart and has a great hunger and desire to get back on the battlefield and rejoin the fight!

How did you go about making sure the story flows?

That takes real attention every single day. Each day you have to kind of look and go, okay, are we streamlining? Are we still on the path? What is the broader message of the movie? Are we thematically kind of in line with what we started out wanting to do? And that does sort of veer off the course at times, which can be good and bad. Ultimately, it's just about trying to service each moment truthfully, having it have a continuity, and then just crossing your fingers because you can have the

same ingredients, the same attention and the same sort of commitment. And it just turns out totally different. A lot of the process involves just trusting that everyone is doing their bit. It's not my job to police everyone, but I think in a collaborative space you all want to have each other's backs. So, if I wonder if the plot elements add up story wise, plenty of people can come to me and say whether they think those plot points are correct for Thor. That sense of collaboration was what is so fun about it. It's the sort of set that Taika Waititi welcomes and embodies himself. The process of making a movie like this is just a constant exploration. Everyone's on the same page basically trying to head in the same direction.

Is being a part of the Marvel Cinematic Universe like being part of a family?

It's cool, because you never know when you are potentially going to get a call or the invite to appear in someone else's franchise or in a mashup of different characters and so on. For many of us, we have been

17 Thor shows off his athleticism in the heat of battle!

18 Hemsworth and Chris Pratt take a break during shooting.

playing these characters for over ten years. For so many years I went from filming to the press tour to more filming to the press tour and so on. It was just like this never-ending thing in the best way.

What aspects of the film are you most excited by?
I'm very excited by the romantic comedy element to it. I think it's a unique angle for this genre and it it's certainly unique to Thor and the *Thor* universe. So, I was really excited to see that all sort of come together and align with the wackiness and the comedy and the sets and the huge universe and world that has been already been established. I feel like we visited more kinds of planets and spaces and environments in this film than kind of any other. So it's pretty exciting.

Is working with Taika Waititi as much fun as it seems?
He's like a big kid! He's like a sort of genius child. His imagination is second to none. He is fascinated by new ideas or gets caught up in something or something that makes him laugh or it's this comedic element that he wants to throw himself into. There's never a dull moment when you are working with Taika. I just love working with him. We have a great thing going. From the very first time we worked together, it was about kind of doing something new and not getting put in a box and not being stuck in one lane. Marvel Studios' *Thor: Love and Thunder* follows that ethos. Taika and I have become great friends, and outside of work, we spend a lot of time together. ⦿

"There's never a dull moment when you're working with Taika... He's like a big kid!"

19 Chris Hemsworth on set with (from left) Tessa Thompson and Natalie Portman.

NATALIE PORTMAN
JANE FOSTER
THE MIGHTY THOR

Returning to the Marvel Cinematic Universe for the first time in nine years, Jane Foster's life undergoes some bizarre and unexpected twists and turns.

What was the draw of joining the Marvel Cinematic Universe?

I was excited to work with Kenneth Branagh on a big Super Hero movie, particularly one that's inspired by Norse mythology. It just seemed like someone with this Shakespearian background would have a really interesting take on it. Then, of course, *Thor* went in this unexpected direction now with Taika Waititi at the helm. It was exciting to come back with a completely different lens on the same sort of world.

What was it like working with the cast on the first *Thor* film?

It was incredible being introduced to such enormous talents like Chris Hemsworth and Tom Hiddleston in the early days as they established their Marvel Studios characters. To see such great actors before the world gets to see them is rare and incredible, especially when they are that caliber. So that was amazing. And then, of course, to work with Kat Dennings and Stellan Skarsgaard, who I worked with on a number of scenes in the first two films, had a great sense of energy.

Marvel Studios' *Thor: Love and Thunder* reunites you with Chris Hemsworth.

It's just incredible to watch Chris' talent, and he's just so agile with moving from serious scenes to extreme comedy. He has incredible comedic talent and he has such a quick brain for changing things up, assimilating information, reacting in a creative way, and coming up with new ideas. He's just so committed and works so hard. It's really impressive to watch him work. I always have to remind myself that I have to act in a scene and I can't just be an audience.

Can you describe Jane's journey?

Jane is a scientist who almost needs help being saved by Thor in the beginning to seeking her own solutions and taking her own journey alongside Thor. They're a team, but she's seeking her own path.

What did you think when Taika Waititi pitched the story for Marvel Studios' *Thor: Love and Thunder*?

Taika came over to my house to talk to me about it. I had not been in the last film, Marvel Studios' *Thor: Ragnarok* which was so wonderful and had really enjoyed watching it. When he talked to me about coming back, he told me about how Jane would be The Mighty Thor. It was interesting to consider what that experience could be like. The process of working on a film with Taika is so exciting because it's so improvisatory and just keeps you on your toes all the time. And so it seemed like it would be a really exciting challenge.

▶

01 (Previous spread) Natalie Portman returns as Jane Foster AKA The Mighty Thor.

02 Jane Foster discovers the reassembled Mjolnir.

03 Portman and Taika Waititi share a light moment on set.

04 Chris Hemsworth, Taika Waititi, and Portman review their work.

05 The Mighty Thor and King Valkyrie team up.

▶ **Was working with Taika Waititi an interesting experience?**
It's always really fun working with Taika. He's entertaining on and off camera. Even when we're not rolling, he's always trying to make everybody laugh. He's the life and soul of the party. He's DJing and making jokes and using his microphone to come up with silly things to say to people while we're just setting up for the next shot. So it's such a good energy and it keeps everything really loose and silly and fun. I don't know how he has the energy for it because he does so much. This movie is on such an enormous scale and takes so much work to direct but he really does keep the energy flowing in a creative and fun way.

Did you have fun hitting both the comedic and serious moments?
I think Taika is really good at reflecting the way life can be dark and comedic all at once. You know, most of the time, when we're in our darkest moments, we try and deflect it with humor. Or it's absurd, so it's funny because the darkest parts of life are completely absurd. So I think he really knows how to find that and how important the silly is when the world is falling down. There's always the fact that in something serious there will be light, and in something silly, there will be something dark. It's really extraordinary because it's such a dangerous balancing act and such a difficult one to pull off. But he manages it somehow.

How does Jane become The Mighty Thor?
She decides to go to New Asgard and find Mjolnir. It manages to arrive in her hand, meaning she's worthy. We don't really know why she's worthy, but she becomes The Mighty Thor when it's in her hand.

Did you like wearing the costume?
It's very silly to have both of us be in the same cape, and especially when you see the stunt doubles and the stand-ins also in their capes. There's just a lot of people in capes standing around. But it's also really great to get to share the mantle of Thor.

Christian Bale's performance as Gorr is intense. Was he as scary during the filming?
Gorr is a terrifying villain. He's very scary. All of us were actually a little bit scared.

What does Tessa Thompson bring to the film?
Tessa is such a brilliant, kind and ferocious actress. It's been really fun to get to work with her again. It's been really fun to see her sword wielding skills and, of course, her kinging. So we had a lot of fun getting to show the sisterhood on screen, in battle. ▶

05

06

> "It was really fun to get to train, for the first time in my life, to be really strong."

▶ Why was working with Korg, voiced by Taika Waititi, particularly special to you?

It was very exciting getting to work with Korg, who is my kids' favorite character in the whole Marvel Cinematic Universe. That got me some points at home. It was impressive to see Taika being able to hop in and out of directing and acting in a scene and how he's able to come up with so many things in character and, of course, as the director.

The film utilizes The Volume, a method of using "real" backgrounds as opposed to blue or green screen to realize the various exotic settings in the film. What was that like to work with?

Well, it's definitely a huge change to get to work with so many actual visuals as opposed to blue screens. Obviously, we had a lot of blue screen as well, but it does really change things as an actor to have an idea of what you're looking at because so often someone will have to describe it to you. That can be hard to work with, even when they can show you a visual reference on a computer. But really, then when you're working, you're working off of a completely blue space. So it requires so much imagination for creating the entire world around you. So it's really helpful to have The Volume, where you could really have a sense of what the world would look like.

The Mighty Thor has a real physicality. How did you prepare for the role?

It was really fun to get to train, for the first time in my life, to be strong. Usually, as women, we're training to get as small as possible. So it's exciting to actually be working towards being bigger. It was a really great experience. I worked with a great trainer, Naomi Pendergast. And then also doing the stunt training with the stunt team was incredible. That was fun. I had never done any real training despite having been in lots of action movies, I'd never really done any fight training or anything like that. It was exciting to do flying, take off's, landings, and that sort of thing.

The wirework helped achieve that sense of swooping around and helping Valkyrie in battle, or just flying in and out of frame. It was fun to look like I'm flying! ▶

06 Portman limbers up for a shot.

07 A behind the scenes shot as The Mighty Thor comes to the aid of King Valkyrie.

08

08 Gorr attacks Thor as The Mighty Thor and King Valkyrie join the battle. Concept art by Andy Park.

"I think there's so much energy that comes from being spontaneous and improvising."

Did you work closely with the costume department?
Mayes (C. Rubeo, costume designer) was absolutely incredible. I'm such a fan of her work, and I was so excited to get to work with her. She just has such an extraordinary eye for design. And, yeah, we started fittings really early on this, like compared to how often and how early I normally do fittings. And she was so wonderful and really listened to your feedback of what felt good so that I could move right. And that it wouldn't be too restrictive so that I could do the stunts I needed to do and that Jane felt like, when I was in Jane character, that it felt like someone specific and that it was this kind of specific character, as well. And it was really cool. Her whole team, first of all, they're such incredible artisans. But also, many of them I'd worked with on *Star Wars* 20 years ago here. So that was a nice revisiting a lot of wonderful people.

Did you work closely with the hair and makeup teams?
So Luca and Matteo had done Chris' hair and makeup before when I worked on Marvel Studios' *Thor: The Dark World*. But I didn't work with them then. So it was so great to get to work with them for the first time. They're such wonderful people and so incredibly talented. So, yeah, it was fun to have my long, blonde hair and the different looks that we did.

How was it wielding Mjolnir?
It was great getting to fight with Mjolnir. It definitely, I think, changed the way I moved to like be holding it in my hand. And, of course, really had like a very specific fighting style and everything because of having Mjolnir.

Is it exciting working with Taika's very impromptu type of filmmaking?
I think that there's so much energy that comes from being spontaneous and improvising. And it's definitely intentional. It definitely feels intentional that he wants to keep everyone fresh in that way 'cause there is something like when you have even when it's really funny, when it's written, sometimes when you say it it feel like rehearsed or stale or something when you do it. And when it's different every time, you do feel that energy of like trying to make someone laugh and everyone kind of like almost cracking up all the time.

There seems to be a lot of camaraderie among the cast.
Yeah, I think it's definitely been a really fun like happy set. Everyone's been laughing a lot and enjoying each other. And I think that comes from the top, really. Taika's so funny and so warm and so open and genuinely like caring and creating this really, really nice environment.

09 Jane Foster pays a terrible price for taking on the mantle of The Mighty Thor.

10 In disguise at the court of Zeus.

11 The Mighty Thor.

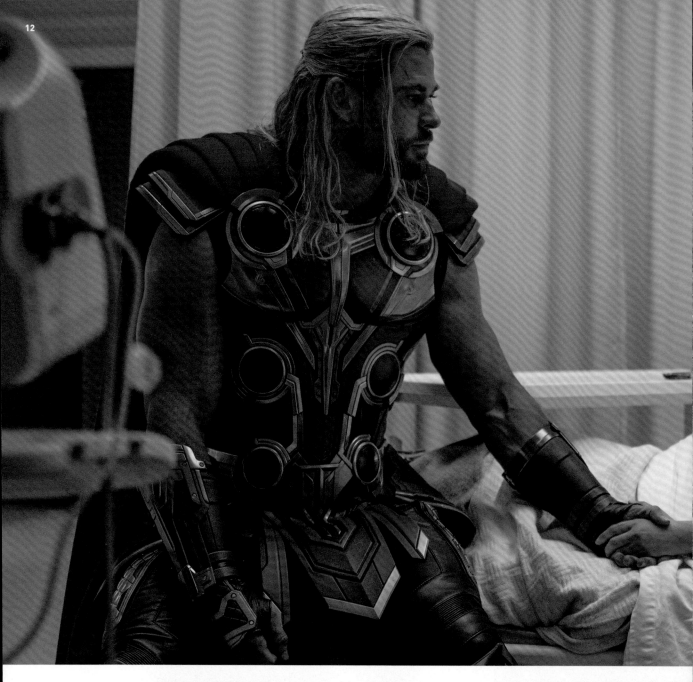

12 Thor lends his support as Jane faces a personal battle.

13 Portman and Hemsworth film against a backdrop provided by The Volume.

14 The heroes plan their next move as Zeus addresses his people.

15 Portman underwent a training regime in order to play The Mighty Thor.

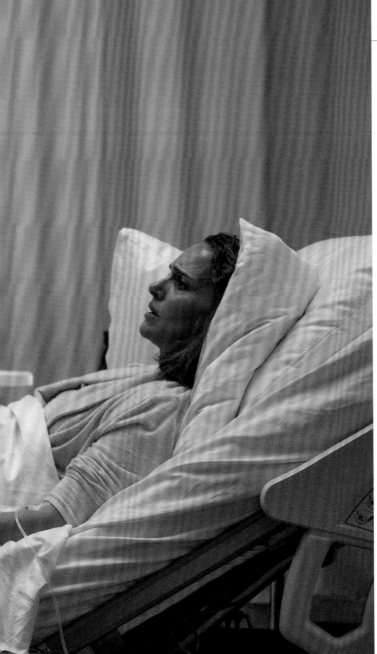

▶ **What was it like to film the scene in the Goat Boat?**
Yeah, we shot that on The Volume, and while it was moving we all had motion sickness all day. Like you'd get off the boat, and you would still feel like you were moving. It was like a bad case of sea legs. Anyhow, that scene was a very wild mix of the most serious conversation on earth and the most out there conversation in space.

There are a number of different genres in the movie. What are your favorite aspects of the movie?
I like that it's a funny, moving and exciting experience because I feel like it has like all of those elements in spades.

What was the biggest challenge and greatest moment?
I think the most difficult and the greatest were probably the same. It went from really silly jokes to really extreme serious emotion back to silly jokes. It just felt really kind of like radical how much we were shifting, and I was really scared about doing it. I really didn't know how to manage it. I didn't know if I could or if we could. Thanks to Taika and Chris I discovered it was possible and that wasn't totally insane to try. It feels really rewarding, I think, when you're that scared but the work pays off. ☻

TESSA THOMPSON

KING VALKYRIE

Now the King of New Asgard, Valkyrie finds her new responsibilities aren't quite as thrilling as her previous life.

What originally drew you to the character of Valkyrie?
I think getting to play a Super Hero that bucked convention and to play someone that was so strong and resilient. The thing that really excites me about the universe in general is even if you're not a hero, if you're a villain, the idea is that your superpowers are the things that have happened to you, either your traumas, the things that people might say that you're different because of the things that might make you ostracized are also the things that make you spectacular and special. I just felt like Valkyrie had that in spades, and the opportunity to get to bring her to life—a character that doesn't necessarily look like me in the comics—was a tremendous challenge.

Can you talk about the evolution of the character?
When we first met her, she had a bit of a drinking problem. She didn't really have much that she felt like she wanted to live for, besides what was at the bottom of a bottle. She didn't have a huge sense of purpose, but she found that again by finding a team. She was someone that was struggling with a lot of guilt and pain. This time around you get to see her rediscovering this sense of purpose outside of what she's always known, which is to fight. You get to see her serving her people as King of Asgard in this new Asgard, which is a new normal, essentially, for her. I think that her arc is one of really discovering why she is on Earth, what she must live for, and discovering who her community is.

What is the philosophy of Asgard?
The thing about Asgard is it has always been said that Asgard is not a place but it's people. It's people have been displaced since the last time we saw them. In the previous movie, Ragnarok destroyed Asgard as they knew it, and they must find a new home, which is on Earth. And I will tell you after having spent a number of days on the set of New Asgard, it is a place I would take a vacation at. It is a little seaside town, somewhere in Norway.

Asgardians are doing what they do best, hanging out in seaside mountain gear, basically. Valkyrie is their king, and there's not much to do until suddenly something happens. It's sort of a sleepy, quiet town, a place you'd love to saddle up with friends and spend a weekend. And then, of course, because Asgardians have it hard, drama befalls them. So they have to figure it out, but we're resilient bunch, us Asgardians. So that's a good thing.

You seem to have a real rapport with Chris Hemworth. Why do you enjoy working with him so much?
I think the most rewarding part of working with Chris on this film has been how big he is now. I'm in awe of how he did it. I thought when we made the last movie that he was the largest human that I have spent time with, and now he's bigger than that. That's been tremendous to see. But, no, it really is inspiring because he just works really hard. I think, also, getting to see someone who's played a character for so long but is constantly reimagining what this character can be is exquisite to work alongside. We have so much fun together. It's amazing to work with someone that cares so much about what they do, and cares so much about a character, and is brave enough to try things and see what sticks and is also a very buff human. ▶

Did you enjoy having Natalie Portman return as Jane Foster?

Jane Foster joins us but becomes the Mighty Thor. It's a gift to see Natalie again. We've worked together before and are good friends. To see her as a Super Hero inside of this universe, which is new for her, is so fun and reminds me of when I'd first joined the universe. It's really fun to get to witness her becoming a hero and to see her rediscover and reimagine who Jane Foster is inside of this new universe that we're setting up.

In general it's really rare to get to share the screen with other women. Sometimes you're the only one. In this case, I think it's impactful, particularly because Jane Foster is a character that doesn't start off as Super Hero. She starts off as a scientist who has a sense of purpose but is sort of breaking out of her own boundaries and discovering things that she's capable of that she didn't know she could do . Her journey is hugely inspiring and something that people can connect to. What Natalie's doing and what Jane Foster gives her the opportunity to do as The Mighty Thor, is to be charmed and surprised by her own power. In that way, I feel like that's sort of how the audience can feel. It was like if you suddenly woke up with superhuman strength, that would be kind

of a trip. It's really fun to get to see her play with that and has reminded me that this is such a cool thing that we get to do as actors, to get to play and have swords and spaceships, and ride on winged horses. It really is something that should make you giddy like a kid. And if it doesn't then you're probably doing it wrong!

What does Taika bring to the set?

Taika is a maniac. I don't think I'm saying anything new. Everyone knows that. It's so cool because, Taika brought such a new energy, not just to the Marvel Cinematic Universe but certainly to this franchise. I remember on Marvel Studios' *Thor: Ragnarok* we would wonder if we would ever work again after this! So, getting to make this new installment feels like bringing the gang back together. Taika is just so inventive, hugely imaginative, and fun. At this point it feels like working with an old friend and a family member, which is, a gift.

Do you like the combination of having fun but also hitting the dramatic beats?

Yeah, sometimes it feels like we'll be having so much fun, and then we must remember the danger

01 Tessa Thompson as King Valkyrie. (Previous spread)

02 Thompson takes a break with Chris Hemsworth, Natalie Portman, and director Taika Waititi.

the heroes are in. So I would say on this film, and certainly in the shooting of it, it feels like moments of comedy careen into moments of drama. Everything is a balance, which, for me, is exciting because that's how life is. I have been really surprised. I thought, particularly for Valkyrie, who in the last film was really contending with the pain of losing her sisters, I was surprised by a moment that I got to play with Gorr of getting to really express that pain in a way that I wasn't as a character able to express it even on the last one when that pain was even arguably more present. And that was a moment of real drama and gravitas that surprised me. I think that there has been a lot of that. I feel like this film has a real balance of heart and sincerity and then, of course, ridiculousness.

How did you prepare for the role?
I did a lot of physical preparation, a lot of reps and ate certain kinds of food and carbohydrates into my face. And then I've also done a lot of research. No, I actually have worked out a lot. I got really strong, which is the gift of doing a film like this. On the last film I had never really done action in this way.

> ## "I feel like this film has a real balance of heart and sincerity and then, of course, ridiculousness."

So it was so much about learning how to wield the sword and using my physicality. For Marvel Studios' *Thor: Love and Thunder* , I had done that before, so I felt really comfortable with the stunt portion of it. I just wanted to push myself to get even stronger than I was on the last time, so it's like doing all that work that no one sees. I mean, hopefully, you can see it in my biceps. But there was a lot of weight training on this one, which I did some on the last but it was a lot more on this one. I was just focusing on endurance and running a as much as possible and not eating a lot of carbohydrates, which was challenging for me.

▶ How has your costume changed?

What's fun for me is that I love a costume change, so I get to also be in civilian clothes. You see her as king wearing these sorts of suited kingly looks. And then you get to see her in her pajamas, which I love because when have you ever seen a Super Hero in pajamas? But Super Heroes have to sleep sometimes! Then there's a change in sort of what you think of as the hero armor, and in her hair, which is exciting bcause it just all coincides in a great new look. I think its really interesting in these films to see the way in which characters evolve in their costumes. Mayes C. Rubeo runs one of my favorite places to hang out on set because it's such an incredible amount of work building these costumes and uses so much imagination. They create amazing costumes not just for the heroes that you see but everyone in the background and the foreground. The costumes for this film are really incredible, the way that they express character and give you a sense of place, the craftsmanship, and just how much time they take over the outfits is remarkable. I'm always just wowed and awed by the work that people do here.

What's going on with the goats?

I don't know. I couldn't tell you what's going on with those goats in a boat. Somehow, these goats were acquired. I had a boat. Together, they make a Goat Boat. Personally, I'm a really big fan of goats. Goats mean a lot to me. This is verifiable on the internet. So, for me, the biggest thing when I read the script was that the goats were officially entering the Marvel Cinematic Universe. And it's about time. There are so many conversations about diversity, but nobody talks about how goats deserve to be represented on screen. And it's high time. I'm happy for goats everywhere and for goat lovers everywhere like me. I actually asked Jake Morrison, our brilliant VFX supervisor if he would put me in my own dedicated shot with the goats. I don't think it's in the movie. But it's one of my most beloved days on any set anywhere.

Was it fun working with Christian Bale and what do you think of Gorr?

Gorr is cool. You're supposed to hate the villain, but I'm kind of team Gorr, which is crazy because I'm supposed to be fighting him! But he is mesmerizing, and he's so cool to look at. I mean he could stand to work on his dental hygiene. But that aside, he's brilliant. He does that thing that I think Marvel villains do so well in that his villainy comes from pain and trauma that he hasn't processed. So it makes him, in a way, a villain that you have sympathy for. And then you have Christian Bale, who's a tremendous actor, who comes to this with a sense of both reverence for the character, sympathy for the character, and a sense of play. He's terrifying, he's funny, and he's oddly charming, minus the dental issues. And he looks cool. Yeah, I can't say enough. He might be one of my favorite on screen villains that I've ever seen and Christian has been really lovely to work with. ▶

03 The King of New Asgard opens the "Infinity Conez" store!

04 Thompson and Waititi share a joke on set.

05 Valkyrie charges into action!

06 Although she is now a king with duties and responsibilites, Valkyrie is longing to return to battle.

▶ How was The Volume used?

The Volume is incredible. It essentially takes you into a 360 space. These various places that you're entering, whether it's the Moon of Shame or wherever, you're essentially inside of it. I think as an actor you spend so much time, particularly in these films, on sets that are blue screen or green screen. You're trying to first convince yourself and thereby the audience. The Volume makes it easier because you don't have to imagine what you're looking out onto. You're looking at it, and it's beautiful. The way that it casts light on our faces and onto the costumes feels really immersive. This is the first time that I've worked on it. It feels otherworldly when you're on these sets.

What have been the most impressive set pieces?

I was really blown away entering New Asgard. It made me chuckle in the script when Valkyrie opens the Infinity Conez store. There were real life Infinity cones on the set. Every single storefront on the set felt like somewhere you could walk into. It all felt so real. It really blew me away. The cobblestone that was built had all the attention to detail, even in the tiny nooks and crannies that the audience might never see. If you're walking around inside of it, you feel like you're transported to this place. I think that's, for me, the incredible thing about working on films like this because you think of all the people that have worked so incredibly hard and for so long. You can really see it reflected when you have those days where there's tons of people on set. I was doing a stunt the other day in New

07 In disguise at the court of Zeus.

08 Thompson on Shadow, who plays the role of Warsong in the movie.

09 As well as appearing in the Marvel Cinematic Universe movie, Thompson also admits to being a fan.

10 Valkyrie's sword, Dragonfang.

"[Valkyrie] loves her people but she's also a reluctant leader."

Asgard and I had like sliced something with my sword. I've learned a new stunt hack, which is when you want to get out of the shot, you just run out of it so that you don't have to be in the background expending energy! When I did that, I went into this other little part of New Asgard that I had never seen with this incredible set dressing. All the extras were doing this brilliant thing where they were passing each other pails of water. I'm not even sure that you can see this in the final movie, but it was a whole enclave and world of people working so hard and working with such authenticity. So I think that's been the tremendous thing, as incredible as it is to see advances in technology. I think what's exciting is when you can match that with also practical just work that takes labor and hands and people. That's been something that's so exciting on this because I think we have a real mix of that. We have cutting edge technology, but we still have hundreds of people that are working or hundreds of hours to make something feel real. And that is just incredible to get to work around.

What are your other memories from the set?
It was so sweet when all the children were on the set. There was this girl, who was beautiful, and she was saying she was in for a fitting, and it had been maybe her fifth or sixth fitting. I got to see pictures of how the character had evolved and what the references were and how much detail had gone into her costume. And that might be a small in a frame. The truth is that you can only do it in these kind of films because you have the wherewithal. So to me, the magic is that you have people at the top of their game with the resources to dream big and to make it happen, whether it's a set piece or a costume.

Is riding horseback something you enjoy?
It is becoming a new passion. Something that was very exciting to me when I read the script is that Warsong would be in this movie because last time you saw Valkyrie, you saw Warsong, but you saw Warsong in the context of a flashback where you see her sisters die, and she become the last of her kind. It's beautiful and tremendous, and we shot with a real horse. And then, of course, the VFX gave the horse wings. But this time we really get to see the emergence of Warsong. It meant hours and hours of training on the horse. Also my incredible stuntwoman Tara Mackin has done such a tremendous job because she's really doing some of those tricks and really riding the horse. She had ridden a little before, but this time she's become a very gifted ▶

10

11 King Valkyrie takes time to reflect as Korg looks on.

12 Behind the scenes on the blue screen set.

13 Filming a sequence aboard the *Aegir*.

"Many of us are Marvel Studios fans too. I'm a fan. I have my favorite characters."

▶ rider. I have not done quite as much because they won't let me. But, now, I'm very eager. I went rogue and decided I wanted to run with a horse, and so I did that on vacation. So when I came back I convinced Graham Ware Jr., who is our incredible trainer, to let me run on the horse. And so I've been doing a lot of that and have just really fallen in love with it. Our incredible horse Shadow, who has been training for months and months, and who also appeared in the last film is back.

Was there anything else you've had to learn for this movie? The horse was really the new thing, and figuring out this new side and personality of Valkyrie as king and what that means to her. She loves her people, but she's also a reluctant leader. She has a hard time with the paperwork and all that admin suff. Thor is spending time meditating outside of his Super Hero duties, and he's really trying to give up fighting. And then, of course, he's thrust back into battle. People ask me sometimes what you would be if you weren't an actor. No one thinks about what a Super Hero would be if they weren't a Super Hero. So in Marvel Studios' *Thor: Love and Thunder* you get to see that a little bit, which is kind of funny.

Was it good to have the Guardians of Galaxy on set? Yeah, that was so cool. The Guardians came and joined us and were with us for the first two weeks. I didn't get to have any scenes with them, but I visited the set to watch them, which was so fun. The Guardians, tonally, are a little more similar to what we do in these new *Thor* movies. It's a joy to get to see people that have their own family dynamic, their own sort of spirit inside of their franchise come into another franchise and see them adjust. Chris has been working more closely with the Guardians, so they have a rapport, particularly the two Chris's (Hemsworth and Pratt). But, still, it's fun to see them come into our universe and be sort of the new kids on the block inside of the way that we work together. I really love the Guardians, in general. I love those films, so it felt very special to have them inside of our film. I think that's the thing of working inside of the Marvel Cinematic Universe is many of us are Marvel Studios fans too. I'm a fan. I have my favorite characters. And so, the idea of the crossover, the idea that you might get to meet one of those people and work closely with them makes me nerd out! So, in an alternate universe, I would love to have actual scenes with Mantis. But it was very fun to watch Pom Klementieff, who is a friend of mine. ◉

MAYES C. RUBEO

COSTUME DESIGNER

A veteran of numerous projects for Marvel Studios, including Marvel Studios' *Wandavision* and Marvel Studios' *Werewolf* by Night, Mayes C. Rubeo returns to create clothes fit for the gods after her work on Marvel Studios' *Thor: Ragnarok*!

How did this movie differ from your experience making Marvel Studios' *Thor: Ragnarok*?
Well, it's very important to really get yourself immersed in the Marvel Cinematic Universe. Having had the experience of working within the Marvel Cinematic Universe before, I know what it takes to make a movie like this. We really thought that Marvel Studios' *Thor: Ragnarok* was gonna be a very super big movie. But this is triple that! It was a good thing that I did that movie in order to know what to expect from Marvel Studios' *Thor: Love and Thunder*! We really had to take it to another level.

What is like to collaborate with Taika Waititi?
Taika is a very creative person and he is constantly evolving ideas and getting everything to the maximum of the capacity. It's delightful to work with him because he has great energy and is a very happy director who treats people wonderfully well. It's good to get the challenge to create different costumes than you usually have in a fantasy sci-fi movie. We have a very close relationship between my crew, Taika and our Visual Development team.

> "When I create a look, I create that whole look."

How much does wardrobe set up a character?
Every character is telling a story, which has ramifications on the whole story. Each one has a different kind of motivation within the story. For instance, we brought back Jane Foster, who is The Mighty Thor in our movie and has an all-new costume made by our team.

How important is collaboration on a project of this size and scale?
Well, in a project of this grand scale, it couldn't function well if all the creative parts are not interconnected. At least three times a week we had creative meetings with the Director of Photography, Baz Iodine, and with Taika, and with our producers, the creators of this show, Visual Development, production designers, set decoration, and hair and makeup.

When I create a look, I create that whole look, and if it's not cohesive with the character then it's not going to work. So it's like creating a person, and somebody else creates the head. It has to be exactly the same DNA. The only way to get that DNA between all of those creative departments is through communication.

How was working with the hair and makeup teams?
Luca Vannella and Matteo Silvi are the very talented artists in charge of hair and makeup designs. They know exactly what is needed to make Chris Hemsworth into Thor, and know the different styles that he has had before. They brought back all those old-fashioned styles in makeup and hair for Marvel Studios' *Thor: Love and Thunder*. ▶

01 Concept art by
Andy Park showing
Thor's new armor.

02 Chris Hemsworth
dons the costume
on set.

▶ Was Chris Hemsworth heavily involved in creating Thor's costume for the film?

Mayes C. Rubeo: Chris is very involved in terms of functionality of the armor he wears. We have to ensure that he has an armor that he can manage in all the very intense actions that he goes through the movie. He needs to be comfortable in it and we have to make sure that he's safe. Creatively, he's also involved because he knows his character so well.

03 The full Thor costume, including the helmet.

04 Concept art by Andy Park.

How many costumes did you create for the film?

Mayes C. Rubeo: We have about maybe five main changes of armor, including the old-fashioned looks that we had in other movies like *Marvel's The Avengers* or Marvel Studios' *Thor: The Dark World*,

All of those costumes came back for us in this movie. On top of that, we were able to design about ten more costumes for him. One of them is the Golden Armor Thor, and this is the most extreme that he has ever been in all the MCU history. ▸

06

▶ Hoiw did the Thor costume inspire The Mighty Thor's armor?.

Mayes C. Rubeo: Jane Foster gets all this energy from Mjolnir. She recharges and becomes a super muscular character. And that's when Thor zaps into the new and improved Golden Armor Thor.

The Mighty Thor is a female version of Thor, therefore we took details from the Thor costume and incorporated them into hers. We went back to the old comic books and got that vintage feeling for it. We adapted the helmet and mask to the beautiful face of Natalie Portman, but we didn't want to hide her eyes and features too much.

05 The Mighty Thor, concept art by Andy Park.

06 The Mighty Thor costume.

07 A dynamic piece of concept art by Andy Park.

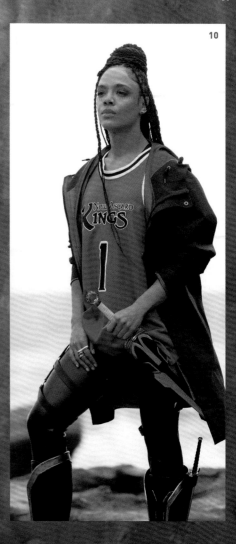

What was the inspiration for King Valkyrie's wardrobe?

Mayes C. Rubeo: Valkyrie is a humble god who wears functional clothes. She has a civilian wardrobe and doesn't wear a crown. In fact, her attire is not like that of a typical queen or a king. She's still a fighter. She's still a warrior. Her clothes reflect that attitude.

08 Concept art by Jana Schirmer showing Valkyrie, the King of New Asgard.

09 Valkyrie's finished costume.

10 Valkyrie's clothes reflect the character's civilian wardrobe.

11 Gorr's eye-catching white robes single him out as a distinctive villain.

12 A close look at Star-Lord's costume.

13 The Guardians' costumes were adapted from the work of Judianna Makovsky who designed the clothes for the *Guardians*' films.

14 Drax and Star-Lord.

▶ **What inspired Gorr's look?**

What is scary about Gorr is what is inside him, and how that reflects in his appearance. What you see on the outside of him is what he's feeling inside. This a lesson for how we feel, how we project ourselves when we have angry feelings. Taika and I talked a lot about how to make this villain important and different. We wanted to stay away from the cliché of a villain wearing black. Because he comes from the shadows, we made him distinctive by dressing him in a white tunic. He steps out of the shadows, but you barely see it until he's in front of you thanks to the genius of our Director of Photography, Baz Iodine.

14

12

13

14

15

Was it fun to work with the Guardians of the Galaxy?
I had the great honor to design a costume for each of the Guardians of the Galaxy. It's something that I had always dreamt of. It's a tribute to what my wonderful colleagues have made for them, especially the great Judianna Makovsky, who created all of the costumes for Marvel Studios' *Guardians of the Galaxy Vol. 1*, Marvel Studios' *Guardians of the Galaxy Vol. 2* and *Marvel's The Avengers*. So I followed on from what she had done and made my own adaptation. ▶

▶ **Is it a challenge to create clothes for aliens?**

I often create costumes for worlds that don't exist. I created costumes for the Indigarrian people, who are a race of very noble people that live in peace, ruled by King Yakan. He's a beautiful venerable character. They have great architecture and great costumes. They are a little bit of a two-level society. There is the entourage of the king and then the rest of the people who are farmers.

The challenge was creating something new. We created a variety of costumes, and every single costume is different. Every person that is in the movie is an individual and I have to make them look unique. We made these costumes, treating the fabrics and changing the colors and painting on top of the color again. We looked for the right shoes for them and found interesting jewelry, crowns, and headpieces.

What inspired the Booskans' outfits?

The Booskans are the hooligans that go ravaging around the world. In this case, they came to bother the Indigarrians. The inspiration behind it, we wanted to have these baddies be different. We created the costumes in complete collaboration with the various departments including Adam Johansen who created these big owl heads with big arms.

The main inspiration for these character was some pictures of biker gangs in New Zealand that Taika brought to my table. I fell in love with the colors and the luster.

Do you work much with the visual effects team?

One of the most important things in my career is that I never stop learning. I have been working with the latest technology. What I learned and what came to affect my costumes is that talking to the Director of Photography and with technicians with ILM, that there was a need of dull many of the metallic surfaces because you don't have the same kind of lighting all the time. So sometimes the Director of Photography will say, "oh, it's too shiny, it's too hot, or it's too dull." So it's like back and forth thing. ◉

16 A biker-gang inspired Booskan.

17 Russell Crowe strikes a pose as Zeus in a behind-the-scenes shot.

MATTEO SILVI

MAKEUP DEPT. HEAD

Matteo Silvi, the makeup designer of Marvel Studios' *Thor: Ragnarok* was responsible for giving the characters a new look for Marvel Studios' *Thor: Love and Thunder.*

How did this movie differ from your experience making Marvel Studios' *Thor: Ragnarok*?
Working with Taika Waititi was definitely one of the most fun experiences of my life. He's such a creative, artistic, fun and crazy director that I wish I could work with him all the time. He gave me a lot of ideas to work on. When we been doing test on characters and different people, he was always giving more details. It's quite a long process, but very exciting.

What were the changes to Thor in this film?
Many of Thor's characteristics have been previously established. For example, Thor carries an eye scar after Marvel Studios' *Thor: Ragnarok*, so we carry that on for his hero look in Marvel Studios' *Thor: Love and Thunder*.

My favorite thing we created was the "Bro Thor" makeup. Chris Hemsworth has to wear a beard and a silicone fat suit, which is really heavy. It weighs about 30 kilos. It's *really* heavy. We also did Ravager Thor, that was new. The makeup was exactly the same look as Marvel Studios' *Thor: Ragnarok* with a different wig. ▶

01

03

▶ **What did you do for The Mighty Thor, as played by Natalie Portman?**
The Mighty Thor has never been seen before. Natalie has quite a few different looks during the movie. When she's Jane, she's got very simple makeup and a wig that looks like her own hair. The Mighty Thor has to look like a heroine, so she needs to be beautiful. I found the inspiration in 1960s style eye makeup. It's just eyeliner to bring up her eyes. There's a big difference when she's Jane to when she is The Mighty Thor.

"I found the inspiration [for The Mighty Thor] in 1960s style eye makeup."

Can you talk about Valkyrie's makup?
We decided to change Valkyrie's look from Marvel Studios' *Thor: Ragnarok* and from Marvel Studios' *Avengers: Endgame*. She used to have some face tattoos in white, but we decided to get rid of them. Taika didn't want them anymore. Also because she's the King of New Asgard, so we decided to go for a different look. For the first scene, when we see her in New Asgard in the middle of the night, we just gave her out of bed look.

We established a few more look for the commercials that we shot in New Asgard when she's wearing a suit. We went for a smoky eye look. That looks great on her. and Tessa was very happy with it. ◉

04

05

06

01 Ravager Thor aboard the Guardian's ship. (Previous spread)

02 Thor in all his glory at the court of Zeus. (Previous spread)

03 An unusual makeup job for Chris Hemsworth.

04 Sif makes a brief return to the Thor franchise.

05 King Valkyrie has a subtly new look in the film.

06 The Mighty Thor shows off her heroine status as she stands by Thor.

LUCA VANNELLA
HAIR DEPT. HEAD

Luca Vannella's career has seen him creating hairstyles for Mark Ruffalo (Hulk) and Chris Hemsworth (Thor), but Marvel Studios' *Thor: Love and Thunder* sees him taking his skills to a whole new level.

What makes Thor in this movie unique?
I've been working on the *Thor* movies since Marvel Studios' *Thor: The Dark World*, and I have also worked on three *Avengers* movies, so I've been following that character quite a long time now. Things change it quite a lot from Marvel Studios' *Thor* where he was more gold blonde and more bleached on his beard and his eyebrows. We changed that to a more of a Viking look and then we kept it through all these movies.

What is working with Taika Waititi like?
Well, he's a a total genius. He's so good to work with and is such a friendly guy. He trusts us. And he wants to push it a bit further with the looks.

How much does the hair say about the characters in the film?
Well, as I say, the look for Thor in this production is "Viking" but the color is more a kind of ash tone instead of a gold blonde. For The Mighty Thor's look, we wanted to have her be blonde as well, but with a darker root.
The idea was that when she gets the armor, she's got short brown hair, and the force of the hammer grows her hair.
For Tessa Thompson, we wanted to keep the same feel as the previous movie on Marvel Studios' *Thor: Ragnarok* that I did, but with different texture. On that movie, she was very straight and sleek because she was living on this planet Sakaar where everyone was so sleek. The set was so shiny, so her hair reflected that.

In Marvel Studios' *Thor: Love and Thunder* she's in New Asgard, this Viking village in Norway, and so we wanted to give her a different feel with braids that are more of a Viking look. We gave her blue hair at the back when she transforms into the armor and goes to battle.

Is Chris Hemsworth involved with developing Thor's different looks?
He plays with the looks a lot. The Ravager look is a leather jacket that gives a rock and roll vibe. It made it look like a rock star more than a Super Hero.

How did you approach Jane Foster's transformation into The Mighty Thor?
So when I had a talk with Natalie Portman for the first time on this movie, I told her my idea to go blonde when she was The Mighty Thor, because I thought, well, even if she's naturally brown brunette, it would be nice to see The Mighty Thor blonde next to Thor with the red cape billowing.

So we started to play with some colors, and because the time passed from the last time that we saw Natalie in Marvel Studios' *Thor: The Dark World*. I thought to go a bit shorter, so you see a change. That was the final decision from Taika and the producer and Natalie. ▶

02

"We used more than 200 wigs and many hair pieces and braids which we had to maintain during the course of the shoot."

▶ How much fun to do you have with supporting characters? Yeah, every week we had new people coming on just for one week or a few days. They were fun to do. So we made the hair look like it been weathered. That looked great, but there were so many. We had a team of 20 people just for the cast, plus all the background artists.

Can you talk about the collaboration between departments? When I started on the film I talked to Mayes C. Rubeo, the costume designer, who worked on Marvel Studios' *Thor: Ragnarok* with me. We know each other well and work together well. We share information, and share thoughts on what we are doing. It's always a collaboration. It's the same with the makeup designer, Matteo Silvi. I've been working with him for a long time and so we always trying to design one look together with the hair and makeup so that everything fits. We try to use the same colors, so if Matteo does a blue makeup, I can insert the similar blue coloring into the hair.

What is the size and scope of this movie? We used more than 200 wigs, and many hair pieces and braids which we had to maintain during the course of the shoot. You always need people to keep the hair up to date and fresh, and washed, and re-curl them and reset them. It's a big team effort. ◉

01 The Mighty Thor. (Previous Spread)

02 King Valkyrie rules.

03/04 Star-Lord makes a cameo appearance at the start of the movie alongside Mantis and the other Guardians.

05 Thor shows off his Ravager look!

KYLE GARDINER

STUNT COORDINATOR

Stunt Coordinator Kyle Gardiner is the man
charged with making Thor's adventures as
thrilling and action-packed as possible.

What piqued your interest about working on Marvel Studios' *Thor: Love and Thunder*?
I think, initially, it was Taika Waititi. It's the creative process that he brings to the table. Everything that's on paper never remains quite the same because once he gets his hands on something you never know what he is going to do. I think that's always a big attraction.

What were Taika's ambitions for the action sequences?
With Taika, the action is always very character driven and story driven. It's not action for the sake of action. We always try to design things that keeps the story moving forward and the characters moving forward. As the movie progresses, the fights and the characters also progress, so the action has to progress with it.

How was training with Chris?
Bobby Holland Hanton, an ex-gymnast, is Chris Hemsworth's stunt double. Chris is very athletic, as well, but when you start to carry the extra size that they were, you have to make sure their range of motion is still good and that harness work and things like that are still possible, because everything alters. The physics of things change, so you just have to adapt, and there's a few moments of struggle before you push through and learn to design action sequences with the costume restrictions, and with the performers increased size that they're carrying and everything like that.

What about Natalie Portman and Tessa Thompson?
Natalie came in very early, ready to work. She was on the wires and she was ready to fight. I think it might be her background as a dancer or just her nature in general, but she wanted to master everything as much as possible, so she could do as much as possible. So we made sure we gave her much time as her schedule would allow.

It was much the same with Tessa. Tessa came in ready to go. She was trained, fit and prepared. So I just had to teach the choreography and find the time to get Tessa and Natalie in with the stunt guys.

How do the Visual Effects play into the choreography?
There is a close relationship with the Visual Effects Department and ourselves. I think it's important they have an understanding of what we're trying to achieve, and we have have an understanding of what they're trying to achieve. Things that could be very difficult can become a lot easier when you're working with them knowing what each brings to the table.

What are the challenges involved in incorporating props and weapons?
Safety's a big thing. We all talk about it, but it really is a case of trying to incorporate things that look as real as possible while limiting the potential hazards, risks and outcomes. We utilize the appropriate props including

02

"We like to push the boundries and try and create something that's unique or hasn't been done before."

01 Gorr brandishes the powerful Necrosword. (Previous Spread)

02 Thor finds an original way to keep two of the Booskan bikes at bay.

03 Thor answers the call of the Guardians as he joins the battle.

04 King Valkyrie shows off her skills in battle.

soft weapons and breakaway scenery depending what we're doing and what wire gag or fight piece is neeeded. The setup of having actors versus stunt doubles or even actors opposite each other requires a choice as to what kind of props we need. Having the correct props is a huge demand on a show like this, especially when you've got all those characters and all the creatures to work with. We are constantly on the phone being asked for different things. The ability of the props department to adapt and meet our demands was second to none.

What's the scope of the action on this movie?
We always like to try and reinvent the wheel, but sometimes it's not always possible. We like to push the boundaries and try and create something that's unique or hasn't been done before. But it has to fit in with the story, and I think with this script there was so much scope for imagination and creativity that I just let my great team go for it. I just let the ideas flow

and see what we can come up with. There was a lot of riffing amongst the group. It's demanding on the stunt doubles. It's demanding on the stunt riggers, and it's demanding on production.

What sets Marvel Studios' *Thor: Love and Thunder* apart from other Marvel Studios films?
Its humor. Chris Hemsworth has amazing comedic timing and athleticism, and that combination just puts you on the front foot.

Which sequence are you most proud of?
It's hard. That's like asking you who your favorite child is! We start off with the Guardians of the Galaxy and Thor. That sequence that was so tongue and cheek and fun. Just to see that interaction between two different universes coming together was lovely to see.

What about the Booskans and the snow sequence?
The Booskans are amazing characters. They followed us through the whole show. I guess that you could refer to them like an owl-like creature. We referenced old action films in there, which always adds a nice element. We have a snow sequence, and to be in Australia shooting with actual snow was a first for me! The special effects department blew me away with what they could do with shaved ice and keep it there on the set, which was mind blowing. We had Bobby and Chris tumbling down a big ice hill, so I guess when you're in ▶

▶ an Australian summer and you're falling down an ice wall, that's a bit unique! It's not something I've done before and probably something I won't get to do again.

What about working on the pre-visualization with your team?
We'll get asked to do a sequence. Whether it be with story boards or VFX viz, we'll get together and choreograph something, and then we'll shoot what we reference as a stunt viz. It just gives people a road map from A to B, how to get there, some ideas we might have for shots. We tend to go to another level and add our in-house VFX amongst our team. We've got some great people, Chan Griffin, Anthony Rinna, Alex Kuzelicki, Yasushi Asaya, Jade Amantea, and the list goes on. We try and do everything inhouse and give the studio, the director, and the actors as close to what we think might be a finished product that they can take to camera. Obviously, they'll vary it, but I think it gives a great start point to walk onto set. I think it just lets you be so prepared on the day so that time is not wasted. You can be ahead of the game. ◉

05 Sif trains the young Asgardians including Axl, the son of Heimdall.

06 Behind the scenes as Thor lets the Guardians' do all the work! (Next Spread)

VISUAL EFFECTS SUPERVISOR

Jake Morrison the Visual Effects supervisor and second unit director on Marvel Studios' *Thor: Love and Thunder* discusses the film's groundbreaking visual effects work.

This film utilizes The Volume. What does The Volume do?

Well, we took some inspiration from what they did on *The Mandalorian*, of course, but the way we're using it is in a completely different way. This has completely the opposite application because Taika Waititi, of course, as we know, is an improvisational filmmaker. He wanted to use the Volume as a Swiss Army Knife for lighting. I was keen on that because we do so much effects work in this movie.

Marvel Studios' *Thor: Ragnarok* was 98% Visual Effects. So, the idea that we could take The Volume and use it as a way to light actors with environments but still maintain the control to be able to create the fantastical environments.

It must be great seeing the actors respond to The Volume. I think that's the consensus amongst any of us who've so dipped our toe into the new LED volume world is that while the quality isn't sustainable for like an in camera final (footage), as we call them., it's wonderful for the actors.

01 Thor leaps into action.

02 The Volume is called into action to show the Goat Boat as it travels through the cosmos. (Next Spread)

02

But, I promise you, in every single other film that I've ever done, it's me standing in the back of the stage with a painter's pole with a tennis ball on the end of it or a laser pointer! So for the actors to be able to feel the scale of how big that space is, like they're in this amazing frozen world and just be able to react to it is fantastic. I think it's very freeing because otherwise you're asking them to just inhabit the theater of the mind a little bit too much. This way, not only are you actually lighting them with the world that you're going to put them, but they can also actually mentally inhabit it.

The Volume, frankly, is here to stay, but it's simply going to get bigger. The single biggest challenge we found with it is that right now because you're basically building a room from LED panels and that clearly takes a lot of resources to do that. If you imagine, we're in a sound stage, which probably has a 60-foot ceiling and is 400 feet long. If you imagine that the entire soundstage is coated with those panels, or something futuristically appropriate like that can output the light. So at a moment we can say we're in another world. Literally the entire environment around the actors would change in a heartbeat in terms of the lighting, the mood, and the tone. That's a game changer. The panels only put out a certain amount of brightness so right now, so you can do nighttime, dawn, and dusk. But what you can't do is anything approaching hard sun. So the next step is to do hard sun because you can't do the entire film at magic hour.

In maybe 10 to 15 years, those panels will be able to put out enough light that you might be able to actually represent the sun, in which case then you can not only go on location with the actors but you can bring the location *to* the actors. I think that's something that we're all excited about, especially as everybody's schedule gets more and more crazy. Travel is not always as easy as you think it is, so being able to have all your actors assembled in one place and bring those worlds to them, will be very powerful.

Do you incorporate other elements such as sets?
When I was talking to Nigel Phelps, our production designer, about how he should approach the LED Volume, the main thing I wanted to get across to him is that he shouldn't think of it as anything different to his normal process. He should design the sets and the environments as he would do normally. When you're actually building them, there's a moment where you choose whether to build a set physically or digitally. It's just an art department choice, as in how much do we need to interact with it, because if I'm building a set on which an actor is only going to sit on one side of a table, there's no point in building a 300-foot set around them. That would be a great one to build digitally.

It's very much just a matter of the design that drives the decision to put the stuff in The Volume or not. Its form follows function.

Are any creatures added to The Volume?
We did have some creatures added in the background. Aside from that, we've kept it to really architectural and lighting, bcause I can describe to the actors that this creature or that creature is going to be there.

► **Is everything computer generated or are there practical builds in The Volume?**
We always start with the real world, regardless of what you do. With any computer graphics, whether it's putting it onto the LED Volume or it's putting it onto the finished screen as a render, you start with real things. So if you are building a red brick in the computer, you would go out and find a red brick. You would take photos of it, and then you'd scan it. The world builds up that way. It's only after that when you get something that you know is based upon the real world, you then change it and you make it your own.

How much footage shot in The Volume will not have additional touches added in post?
Some will be in-camera. We've found that with the lens package that we chose for the picture that any of the long lens closeup shots that you have with people where the background is a little soft is very favorable.

How does the interactive light play a part in The Volume?
The interesting parallel here is that if you look back 15 years ago in computer graphics, the way that they were lighting computer graphic objects is if you wanted to make a coke can and put it onto a table, you'd go and shoot the table. Then you'd model the coke can in the computer, and put textures on it, and you'd put it there in the computer. There were these little wire frames of lights that we had to play with back in the day, so you'd be playing with this incredibly primitive tools to light the thing. Years ago, we switched to what we call image-based lighting, which is when you shoot the plate of the table, and you then shoot what we call a light probe, which is putting a camera there and grabbing an accurate representation of all of the light that the object is seeing at that moment and in a very high dynamic range. Then, instead of just reflecting it, we actually project that light on it. So we literally light the coke can, in this case, with the light that we captured from the set. That's what makes the CG look realistic nowadays. We've done that with actors now, so we can take a particular location in the real world steal the light effectively, and bring it to the actor, and then project that onto them to make them feel like they're really there.

How did you approach the Creature and Prosthetics team?
The goats are the heaviest goats ever made! I saw a couple of our crew members carrying them down some stairs and our hearts were in our mouth. Like will they make it?
The wonderful thing about working with Adam Johansen, who heads the Creature and Prothetics department, is that we work very collaboratively. We would start with a design, which will be visual development or VisDev for Marvel Studios, and then we would look at it between Mayes C. Rubeo, Adam and myself. We would look at the character and work out which bit can we do best where? So if

03 Thor and the Guardians feel the heat - thanks to The Volume.

04 Groot and Rocket.

05 Omnipotence City.

06 The two Thors battle Gorr in the Shadow Realm.

07 Thor brandishes Stormbreaker.

08 The Guardians' Ship is held by Thor.

the character was best achieved in costume, Mayes would do it. If it was best done with a prosthetic on an actor, then Adam would take it on. My department would handle it if Visual Effects was the best option. Nobody wanted all the glory, we all just wanted to do what's best for the movie. So everything you see there is completely appropriate. Miek is the perfect example of the collaboration. We knew what Miek looked like and we had the VisDev design that we'd worked with Taika Waititi on. Everybody thought we should just stick Miek in like a gray motion capture suit, which is what everybody does nowadays. If you can't decide you just stick them in a motion capture suit and be done. But I thought we had the right people to do this, and we absolutely did. Mayes came up with this incredible technical fabric, which is this crazy checkerboard. As you zoom in on it, you see more and more checkerboards. Carly Rees, who's our stunt double, plays Miek. She studied the previous movie, so she knows Miek inside and out. She wore the suit, and a blue mask, and absolutely aced it. Then Guillaume DeLouche, our prop master, gave us these cool knives for hands, safe to wear on set. And, lastly, the Visual Effects department built the Miek head. ◉

BRIAN CHAPEK
EXECUTIVE PRODUCER

Brian Chapek returns to work on Marvel Studios' *Thor: Love and Thunder* having served on the production teams of Marvel Studios' *Thor: Ragnarok* and Marvel Studios' *Black Widow*.

Where does Thor find himself at the start of this film?
Thor is now Marvel Studios' longest running franchise character and this is the first time we'd done a fourth solo movie for a character. I think with that there's some expectations to keep building upon his character in profound and meaningful ways. We've seen him grow so much over the years, but after the events of Marvel Studios' *Avengers: Endgame*, we've started to see some cracks in his armor. He started to feel some ownership over all the people that he's lost in his life, and he feels responsible. So we find Thor in a little bit of a dark place, and this movie is very much his fight to get back into being a hero again. After the events of Marvel Studios' *Avengers: Endgame*, Thor has gone off with the Guardians of the Galaxy to have these amazing adventures. We needed to tell that story and deliver on that promise of what does that Thor and Guardians team-up look like. But at the same time, the movie necessitated them going their separate ways because that was the only way for Thor to have his own true adventure. So our hope is that we have the fun of those characters all being together before we thrust Thor on his own journey when he finds out who he is again.

It's extraordinary watching Taika Waititi, Chris Hemsworth, and Chris Pratt working together.
Starting back on Marvel Studios' *Thor: Ragnarok*, we saw what can happen when you get Taika and Chris in a room. They're just so funny and it's so effortless. And then when you throw Chris Pratt, Star-Lord, into the mix it was just a ridiculous amount of fun, and it opened us up to even more humor to explore in this movie.

Why was the time right for Jane Foster to return?
I think with every new installment we do, it's important that we never tread like the same territory. We always have to do something different. We have to do something surprising, and with Marvel Studios' *Thor: Ragnarok*, no one saw that coming. No one knew those movies could be as fun and as bold as *Ragnarok* was. So we had the same challenge on Marvel Studios' *Thor: Love and Thunder*. One of the big keys to that was re-introducing Jane Foster but actually Jane as The Mighty Thor.

I think it was great having Jane in this movie just because of what that means for Thor. We find Thor in a place where he's closed off his heart, and he feels responsibility for losing so many people. He's forgotten to love, and so what happens when you throw Jane back into the mix, especially now that she is The Mighty Thor?

Natalie was super-excited to come back, and most importantly, to portray such an amazing character in the *Thor* comics. Jane is a really interesting character because she's human, but she gets this amazing power. So what happens when she gets that power? How is she going to deal with it?

01 Behind the scenes as Sif warns Thor of the threat from Gorr. (Previous Spread)

02 Thor and The Mighty Thor reunite aboard the Goat Boat.

03 The motion-captured character Korg returns.

04 Chris Hemsworth poses on the blue screen set.

05 Star-Lord and Thor contemplate the future aboard the Guardians' Ship.

Thor has an interesting journey in this movie.
In Marvel Studios' *Avengers: Endgame* we see Thor has lost himself a little bit. He's started to overeat and he's let his heroic days go. Marvel Studios' *Thor: Love and Thunder* needed to tell his bounce back story, which he tells with the Guardians in a montage as they go through space, having these amazing adventures while Thor gets back into the game and into shape.

Chris took it upon himself to be the biggest and the strongest version of himself that he's ever been... and he absolutely delivered. We wanted to see the contrast between Thor that we left off in Marvel Studios' *Avengers: Endgame* and the Thor that we find here.

In some ways, it feels like Chris is always Thor. He's done this for so long that he knows exactly what the character needs to do and what he needs to do to get in shape. It's such a big part of his life and the character that you just let him go with it. You know he's going to show up on the day prepared. ▶

► **Explain the different looks for Thor.**

There are so many amazing looks in this movie, and I think that's a big opportunity for us on these *Thor* films is to see Thor evolve, not only as a character but his looks. If Thor is gonna go up with the Guardians, he must look like a Guardian. And he finds his very own version of that, but in a Thor way. We're always looking to evolve Thor's looks, and they do get progressively bigger and bolder. When The Mighty Thor enters his life, he takes on his most extreme look yet. He dons this amazing over the top armor, head to toe in gold and blue that really hearkens back to the original comics where they didn't hold back in terms of the fun and the color.

How important is Mayes C Rubeo's contribution to the costumes?

Mayes' costume designs are such an integral part of this process because the sheer amount of characters that she needs to develop. This movie has so many different charcters, including   monsters, and Mayes constantly delivers. Coming off of Marvel Studios' *Thor: Ragnarok*, she knows the world and keeps delivering these amazing suits for our heroes to wear.

How was Valkyrie developed?

We find Valkyrie where we left her on Marvel Studios' *Avengers: Endgame*. She's been entrusted to be the king of Asgard, and she's still trying to find her place. She's trying to learn what kind of king she wants to be, but it's not everything she's ever wanted because, first and foremost, she's a Valkyrie, the last remaining one. As she becomes a king, she starts to remember what it was like to have her sisters. She misses the days of being in the battle, and when the opportunity presents itself Valkyrie's first in line to get back into it.

What has The Volume added to the film?

This is the first Marvel Studios film to utilize The Volume, which is this amazing technology that allows you to be completely surrounded, 360 degrees in a digital environment. So it allows you to seamlessly place practical sets with a digital world. It has a lot of amazing benefits, because it gives a fully immersive world for our actors to interact with.

So often in our movies, our actors are imagining what's going be added in the blue screen. The Volume shows them it in real time. So I think it creates an even more heightened performance, and it makes you feel like you're there.

How did you approach topping Loki and Hela as villains?

I think the *Thor* franchise has a history of producing some pretty interesting villains. Loki is one of our best. Hela is one of our best. So it was very important for us to introduce another terrifying villain. We found that in Gorr the God Butcher. He has a big history with Thor in the comics. If you're going to introduce Gorr you need to find someone who's capable of bringing that character to life. And that's Christian Bale.

09

> ## "I think the Thor franchise has a history of producing some pretty interesting villains."

Was it fun to see Korg again?

Taika was very excited to play Korg again. It's amazing how quickly he just like sinks into that character. Taika's directing and doing motion-capture for Korg, and sometimes the two just kind of blend together. You never really know which one is which. Korg is, obviously, a very funny character, but I think he also points out some very important things in this movie that maybe Thor doesn't even recognize in himself. He kind of has this hidden wisdom that maybe only Korg could uncover.

How were the goats brought to life?

This movie is introduces two new, unexpected characters in Toothgnasher and Toothgrinder, our two space traveling goats, which Thor and our team of heroes take along on their journey. You would think something

like that would be completely CG and you'd have no reference, but we didn't do that. We created practical goat heads for VFX reference but more so just to be able to interact with them. After the end of every take you kind of roll these giant goat heads in, and it would just be hysterical. It's really a great proof of concept of how much fun these characters can be when we bring them to life during post-production.

What have audiences connected with in the Thor films?

I think that keeps us having to evolve him, and people need to be surprised. I think the most surprising thing about this movie is that even though it has giant action scenes, and amazing comedy and humor, deep down it's a love story. That was something that we were very passionate about telling and hope that surprises audiences. ◉

06 A different look for Mjolnir.

07 The heroes in disguise as they attempt to infiltrate Omnipotence City.

08 Thor and the Guardians join forces.

09 Nebula and Drax feel the heat of battle.

ADAM JOHANSEN

CREATURE AND PROSTHETIC DESIGNER

Creature and Prosthetic Designer Adam Johansen oversaw some of the more unusual characters in Marvel Studios' *Thor: Love and Thunder.*

Which characters were you responsible for on Marvel Studios' Thor: *Love and Thunder* ?

The Booskans were amongst of the first characters that we worked on. There was a lot of back and forth in order to get them right. They weren't originally meant to be owl creatures. They were warriors with a mask with the real Habooska character underneath. We started designing it, and the more we honed in on the look of the Booskans, the more Taika felt they should be the creatures instead of the masks that the Habooska was wearing. We then added Viking stylings like top knots and eventually took it into the biker kind of mongrel mob look with leathers. And, yeah, I love the Booskans. They were the first ones with the Indigarrians, Toothgnasher and Toothgrinder.

Tell us about the goats.

The goats were from the comics. Talking to Jake Morrison from the Visual Effects department, and Taika, we felt that was kind of important for them to have a presence on set. They were maybe the trickiest thing we did on this show because they're such important characters. We made lifesize versions of them, the size of Clydesdale horses. I only made the head and the neck in order to capture the character

in a static model to be able to have on set. Coming up with a design that was true to some of the early visual development art that we received but giving them the most realistic finish.

The goat team was led by Carla Harrison who did all the synthetic hairs and fur. It was tricky, but they turned out great. I remember the day we presented them to Taika and everyone on set. The goats got a good response and they had great presence!

How did you achieve Gorr's distinctive look?

I saw the design of Gorr in an early visual development meeting and thought it was really powerful imagery. The character, of course, is tragic and intense on every level. However, bringing that into a three-dimensional sculptural place was a great challenge. The makeup process was long as Gorr has got tattoos over his entire body. Christian Bale, who played Gorr, went through a lot. I started off with the scarification on his head cast and presented Taika and everyone with a few different sculptures so they could see them in real life. There's a lot of different scars, like keloid scars. I think we landed at a pretty gruesome spot. He's totally covered from shoulder to hands, chest, forehead, down his back, and feet. ▶

"The makeup process [for Christian Bale as Gorr] started off at four and a half hours."

▶ One of the other things I suggested for Gorr was to keep a hint of the tattoos showing through the scarification. So he's got all these scratched up scars, but you can still see a hint of his past life. We just had to have the tattoos underneath the prosthetics. Of course, he's completely gray. There are multiple colors within that gray, but he is completely painted and has false teeth, full nails, scarification, and coloration. He's a pretty big character. The makeup process started off at about four and a half hours, and we got it down to three and a half as the shoot continued.

Christian was fantastic to work with. Working with him on Marvel Studios' *Thor: Love and Thunder* was one of my favorite collaborations with an actor. We sat down one Saturday, before we started and had a good chat and discussed the character. He was wondering what I was thinking about Gorr and I listened to what he wanted to bring to that character design. He had a lot of great ideas. We worked really hard until Christian was happy that he'd found the character.

Did lighting or The Volume have an impact on what you did with the character?
It did when we were working with The Volume. Talking to Baz Iodine, our cinematographer, we learned that all our characters, the Indigarrians in particular, looked quite different depending on where they were shot. Gorr's gray did read slightly differently. The layers and levels of Gorr were the hardest thing for us. He was becoming more human, losing the gray slightly. It was really tricky finding that balance because he's an alien, he's not human. ▶

01 A close up view of a Booskan. (Previous Spread)

02 A shadow monster.

03 The Booskans go before the cameras in this behind the scenes shot.

04 King Valkyrie's aide.

05 A ferocious shadow monster attacks New Asgard.

06 Johansen's department created a large menagerie of creatures.

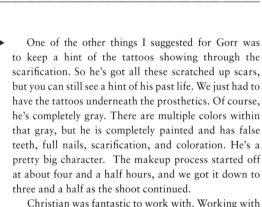

05

06

07

► There were lines and lines of people getting painted blue. It was really a production line when we were working on the Indigarrians. We had some big days on the film when we were working on some really big numbers of creatures. The studio team did a fantastic job, but we found the best way to sort of get those kind of numbers through with the amount of crew that we had was by breaking the team into different sections.

The Indigarrians had brow pieces and cheeks and their big, scared eyes so we had prosthetic applicators who would glue on the pieces and people who were sponging them blue, and people that were spray painting them and powdering them. There was a tent of people going through different colors with their spray guns, building up the layers: blues, beetroots, grays, and speckling. It was something to see when people were walking out of the makeup tent blue! ⊛

08

07 Thor and Korg stand over Falligar, God of the Falligarians.

08 The Wolf Woman seen in the montage sequence was played by Chris Hemsworth's real life wife, Elsa Pataky.

09 A dragon-like creature in Omnipotence City.

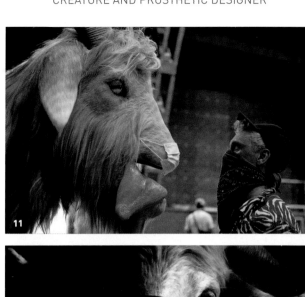

10 Concept art by
Jana Schirmer
showing the
scene-stealing goats!

11 Taika Waititi
inspects a goat head.

12 Korg makes a
new friend.

13 The goats pull
the Goat Boat.

14 The goats aboard
the Guardians' Ship.

PRODUCTION DESIGN

Explore the sets of Marvel Studios' *Thor: Love and Thunder* including the Guardians of the Galaxy's Ship, and New Asgard.

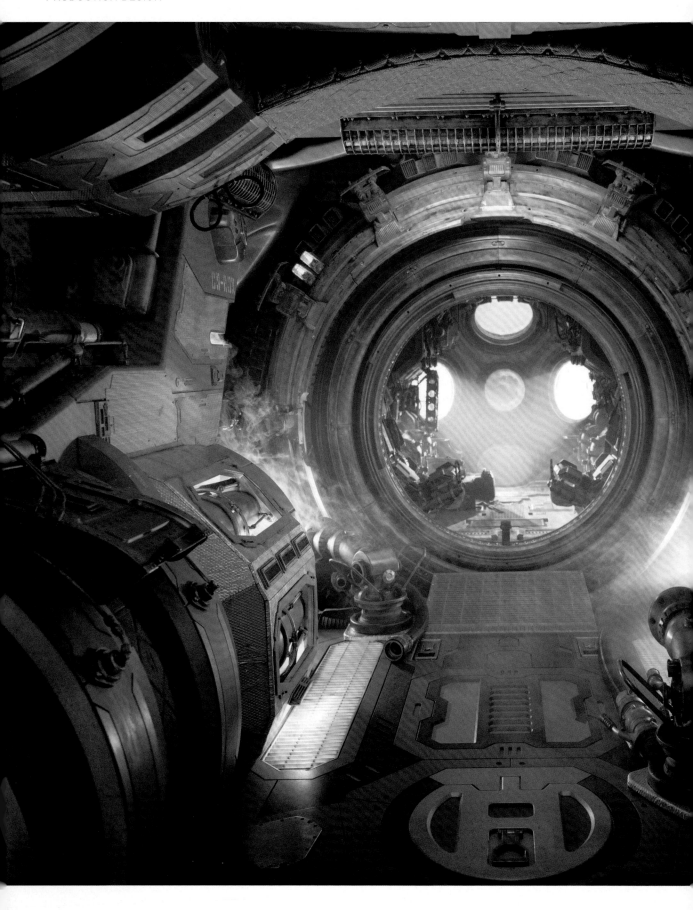

01/02 A look inside the Guardians' Ship.

03/04/05/06 The Asgardian's new home, New Asgard.

TAIKA WAITITI

CO-WRITER / DIRECTOR

The visionary director looks back on reinventing Thor in Marvel Studios'
Thor: Ragnarok and taking him to new heights in Marvel Studios'
Thor: Love and Thunder.

How would you classify your interpretation of Thor?
Well, I felt like I wanted to focus more on Chris Hemsworth as being the character. In the first two films, I found Thor interesting, but I didn't feel like enough of Chris was coming through in that characterization. So, that was the main focus really because I think Chris is such a sensitive and caring person. Whenever you hang around with him you very much feel in good hands and that you're being taken care of. I think that's what an audience wants when they're in the presence of a Super Hero. They want to feel that sense of comfort and ease that they're being looked after when they're going on these wild rides. We really focused on getting much more of Chris' personality and energy into the character of Thor.

There was a shift between the second and third films. Were you interested in playing with different film genres?
Yeah, well, that's right. One of the cool things about the Marvel Studios films is this ability to embrace and skirt around these various genres within the film. Sometimes it might feel like a heist movie and other times it will feel like more of a comedy. Other films will feel very dramatic, where the stakes are very high and everything's very serious. Or you might get a political thriller. What's great is it keeps audiences guessing all the time, so it's always more interesting to see these characters within these different genres so that they themselves feel different as well.

Were you concerned about torturing Thor too much?
I think it's great because he's essentially a god and feels very much indestructible. He can fight the Hulk and still survive. I feel like you can see him go through a lot more than what other characters would go through. It seems like he can handle the knocks a lot more. And so, it didn't ever really feel like it was too much. I think one thing we would always look out for is that it didn't feel like he was always on the back foot or wasn't capable of doing things.

He's smart enough to figure out a way out of a situation or to find an intelligent solution to something rather than always just fighting his way out. So, that was important to us. But, after getting that haircut and losing the hammer, I did wonder if blowing up his planet was maybe one step too far...

Were you anxious about the reaction?
I felt really confident and happy with the direction we were pushing Thor into with being better with the wisecracks and more charming. He just felt like more of the kind of hero that I wanted to follow. He sometimes swings first and asks questions later. But he has this innate sense about him that you want to keep watching him and you'll follow him into any situation because he's got your back.

Were you surprised at just how popular Thor became with Marvel Studios' *Thor: Ragnarok*?
I think now and then sometimes, whether it be fans or just people who were used to something, fear change. They don't like the idea of changing the character or changing their personality. But, speaking personally from experiences in real life, people do change all the time. And certainly people's personalities are always changing So, I don't think it's very far fetched to expect that of a character like Thor, who has been around for thousands of years, to evolve. So there's time for him to change and go through different phases. He probably went through his emo phase! So, I wasn't really worried. I was definitely relieved when I knew how high he was testing in the preview screenings. Even in the *Avengers* screenings I'm pretty sure he tested really, really high. Even more than relief, it was just a sense of pride that we'd managed to create something new and reinvent this character in a way that made the film really succesful but also made people want to see more of him over and over again. It gave Chris more of a sense of ownership over the character.

▶

▶ Was there a story you were trying to tell before you handed it off to the Russos [the directors of Marvel Studios' *Avengers: Infinity War* and Marvel Studios' *Avengers: Endgame*]?

I think once the film came out there wasn't any discussion as to whether we'd do another one because I think everyone just wanted to see what would happen with the film. I was always very keen to come and work with Marvel Studios again just because I had such a good experience. I think we all collectively felt like we should take a turn around the garden once more and take Thor out for another adventure. We talked very briefly I think a few months after it premiered about trying to make something happen.

You had to see how things shake out at the end of Marvel Studios' *Avengers: Endgame*.

Yeah, I mean, I was relieved that he was alive at the end of that because it would've made my job harder.

What's left to do to Thor?

What is left to do to him? It's got to be something that feels like it's carrying on with the evolution of the character, but still in a very fun way and still giving him things to come up against that feel like they're building on the obstacles that he has to overcome. I don't think we can have a villain that's weaker than Hela. I feel like we need to step up from there and find a villain that's somehow more formidable.

Is it fun to twist the genre even more in Marvel Studios' *Thor: Love and Thunder*?

I think this movie feels really similar to *Ragnarok* in terms of the tone and style. I think we probably just doubled down on how vibrant and crazy the worlds are and the situations we put him in.

Marvel Studios' *Thor: Love and Thunder* was a very loud and bombastic film, and we wanted to keep going with that because when you're dealing with a space Viking, that already suggests that the movie is going to must be over the top and really in your face. The combination of space and a Viking is already so ludicrous and kind of ridiculous that if you run at that and embrace

01 Taika Waititi behind the camera during the principal photography for Marvel Studios' *Thor: Love and Thunder.* (Previous Spread)

02 Waititi dons the motion capture suit to play Korg opposite Rocket. (Previous Spread)

03 On set with the Guardians of the Galaxy.

04 A rare moment of calm on the busy *Thor* set.

it and use that as the thing that powers the story-- Then you can come up anything you want, and you're only really limited by your imagination.

Was it important to have a wide range of familiar faces?

We've got Korg and Valkyrie. Natalie Portman is in the film. And Meik, the insect creature. And then, of course, we have all these other characters that we created, which was really fun. Gorr, the villain, comes from the original Marvel comic books.

Was it exciting to Natalie Portman back in such a dynamic way?

It's exciting that I get to retain Thor as himself and continue that journey with Chris, who I love working with. And then I get to bring in this character that's been established before, Jane Foster, who disappeared in Marvel Studios' *Thor: Ragnarok*. I think what's great is the fans probably never thought they'd see her again. We're pulling this storyline from The Mighty Thor comic book arc from Marvel. She becomes Thor and essentially becomes a Super Hero and she and Thor team up. So, that's exciting for me in that I think it's great to see Natalie in a way that we don't expect. She's such a great actor and her appearence here is in keeping with reinventing this franchise again and again, and trying to do something different every time I don't think we want to go back to seeing her in the same role really. We don't want to see her just being a scientist on Earth waiting for Thor. I think it's great that she's more empowered, and she's more motivated. And, independently, she's a very strong character who now is really Thor's match and can do all the things that he can do. The thing that's really cool is to see a female being a god and getting to fly around and do all of these things. It's like Captain Marvel was such a great character just because you get to see a woman doing all of those things that have predominantly been only reserved for male characters in these comic books.

"I was relieved that [Thor] was alive at the end of [Marvel Studios' *Avengers: Endgame*] because it would have made my job harder!"

What are the core elements to Thor?

I think that you've got to pit him against more and more outlandish and crazy beasts, monsters and aliens because it's really in keeping with not only the comics, where he comes from, but also the mythology that he originates from. There's all sorts of insane monsters that they've thought up back in the old days. I think that's very much a Thor thing, really, more than I think any of the other characters in the Marvel Cinematic Universe. I really feel like Thor is the one that lends itself towards big, inventive, colorful creatures and aliens and things from different worlds. I think with that character, especially, you get to travel around those worlds. What's cool about Thor being so old is he's been traveling to all of these worlds and I don't think he's that surprised when he sees these things.

So, there's a fun element to him and he has a casualness and a sort of swagger about him when he visits these worlds and encounters these aliens that I don't think you'd get when it's an earthling traveling through space exploring the universe.

Where do we find Thor at the beginning of Marvel Studios' *Thor: Love and Thunder*?

At the beginning of the film we find Thor in a different state to when we left him at the end of Marvel Studios' *Avengers: Endgame*. So, in the beginning of this film when we find Thor, it's a different version of him again. In this film, we find him in a more meditative state. And he's more contemplative, and he's actually trying to find peace. So, he's trying to figure out ways of dealing with conflict through non-conflict and non-violence. And so, that's already a really great version of him that we haven't seen before. He's a sort of nice, peaceful hippie that I think is a really fun and unexpected version of his character.

05 Chris Hemsworth and Taika Waititi film
▶ against The Volume.

"It strikes me that Thor, out of all of the other Marvel Cinematic Universe characters, has lost the most."

05 Korg, played by Taika Waititi returns.

06 Waititi relaxes on Zeus's throne.

07 Preparing for a take.

08 On set with Chris Hemsworth.

▶ **Thor may be old, but he's still figuring himself out. What's your take on his journey?**
It strikes me that Thor, out of any of the other characters in the Marvel Cinematic Universe, has lost the most. He's lost both parents and his brother. He did lose his hair, but it grew back. He lost his hammer and he lost his home planet. And now his people are refugees and stuck on Earth. After going through all of the trials and tribulations of Marvel Studios' *Avengers: Infinity War* and Marvel Studios' *Avengers: Endgame*, I think the only thing really left for him at this stage is to reflect on everything that has happened to him. The way he deals with it and deals with these ghosts and demons and all this emotional baggage is to try and see it as some sort of big, cosmic joke, where in a way nothing matters because we're all eventually destined to be leaves and dust. I think what he's trying to do is find a way to deal with all that sadness and anger because he's probably realized that resorting to violence and just dealing with your emotions through your fists or by using an axe doesn't really make you feel any better later on. Yeah, it's a little bit of relief while you're fighting and if you're victorious. But then, it's like chasing the dragon: you always want more. And so, he's trying to figure out ways of dealing with all of this trauma through peace and silent meditation.

What made you want to come back and do another Marvel Studios film?
I really enjoyed the experience of making Marvel Studios' Thor: *Ragnarok*, and I really love the people who run that place. I've had such a good experience with Brad Winderbaum, Louis D'esposito, Victoria Alonso, Brian Chapek, and Kevin Feige. I found it a very collaborative environment to work in and really fun. What's great is everyone's open to ideas. The more imaginative and

creative you can get the better it is for the film that you're trying to make. And because the team are all are imaginative and creative as well, it's just like a good meeting of the minds for me. I felt very supported having made the first film, so, I thought I'd love to come and do another one.

What do you hope the fans will take from the film?
The thing fans can look forward to when they sit down and watch Marvel Studios' *Thor: Love and Thunder* is a fun movie that really embraces the spirit of adventure and the spirit of hope and a real enjoyment of being taken on a ride through different worlds with crazy animals and beasts. There's obviously the usual big, spectacular set pieces and all those things. I really feel like we're expanding the universe on this film and making it funnier, more enjoyable, a bigger adventure with more worlds and with even cooler characters, and new characters as well. So, ultimately, it's a really fun adventure with a kickass soundtrack like the last one!

How did you decide on the title of the film?
The title *Love and Thunder* really is the *Thor* title that people never knew they wanted. Another thing I think is great about Marvel Studios is they are always surprising people with these decisions. When we first came up with *Love and Thunder*, it was something that we discussed, and we thought the fans will really freak out about this. It really suggests a lot of what the film is about. There's not necessarily a love story, but love is a huge theme throughout the film. The thunder, I guess, is the effect that love has on one's heart. When you're in love and when you experience any kind of love, it shakes you to the core. And it's also linked heavily to Thor, the god of sparkles!

Where do we find Valkyrie?
Tessa Thompson as Valkyrie was a huge fan favorite in *Ragnarok*. She's a really fun character. When we came up with that character in *Ragnarok*, I was sort of wanting a kind of Han Solo-ish kind of character who was the kind of mercenary who sold people out and did things just for the cash and wanted to disappear on this junk planet. And so, she's reprising the role, but now she has more responsibilities on earth because she's King of Asgard now. She still has that sense of fun and lightheartedness, and also that really fun anger that comes with the character as well.

What about Korg?
The good thing about Korg in relation to all these other characters who are evolving and changing, is that Korg is a very grounding force in the film. Korg has not changed at all, he's still loyal, and he's particularly loyal to Thor. He's still got that nice, sort of innocence about him and that friendly quality, where he always sees the positive in people, and he's a very positive, uplifting presence to have in the film. I think every film needs that. ◉

MARVEL STUDIOS LIBRARY

MOVIE SPECIALS
- MARVEL STUDIOS' *SPIDER-MAN: FAR FROM HOME*
- MARVEL STUDIOS' *ANT-MAN AND THE WASP*
- MARVEL STUDIOS' *AVENGERS: ENDGAME*
- MARVEL STUDIOS' *AVENGERS: INFINITY WAR*
- MARVEL STUDIOS' *BLACK PANTHER* (COMPANION)
- MARVEL STUDIOS' *BLACK WIDOW*
- MARVEL STUDIOS' *CAPTAIN MARVEL*
- MARVEL STUDIOS: THE FIRST TEN YEARS
- MARVEL STUDIOS' *THOR: RAGNAROK*
- MARVEL STUDIOS' *AVENGERS: AN INSIDER'S GUIDE TO THE AVENGERS' FILMS*
- MARVEL STUDIOS' *THE FALCON AND THE WINTER SOLDIER*
- MARVEL STUDIOS' *WANDAVISION*

MARVEL STUDIOS' *LOKI*: THE OFFICIAL MARVEL STUDIOS COLLECTOR SPECIAL

MARVEL STUDIOS' *ETERNALS*: THE OFFICIAL MOVIE SPECIAL

MARVEL STUDIOS' *SPIDER-MAN: NO WAY HOME*: THE OFFICIAL MOVIE SPECIAL

MARVEL STUDIOS' *DOCTOR STRANGE IN THE MULTIVERSE OF MADNESS*: THE OFFICIAL MOVIE SPECIAL

MARVEL LEGACY LIBRARY

MARVEL'S CAPTAIN AMERICA: THE FIRST 80 YEARS

MARVEL: THE FIRST 80 YEARS

MARVEL'S DEADPOOL: THE FIRST 30 YEARS

MARVEL'S FANTASTIC FOUR: THE FIRST 60 YEARS

MARVEL'S SPIDER-MAN: THE FIRST 60 YEARS

MARVEL'S HULK: THE FIRST 60 YEARS

MARVEL CLASSIC NOVELS
- WOLVERINE WEAPON X OMNIBUS
- SPIDER-MAN THE DARKEST HOURS OMNIBUS
- SPIDER-MAN THE VENOM FACTOR OMNIBUS
- X-MEN AND THE AVENGERS GAMMA QUEST OMNIBUS
- X-MEN MUTANT EMPIRE OMNIBUS

NOVELS
- MARVEL'S GUARDIANS OF THE GALAXY NO GUTS, NO GLORY
- SPIDER-MAN MILES MORALES WINGS OF FURY
- MORBIUS THE LIVING VAMPIRE: BLOOD TIES
- ANT-MAN NATURAL ENEMY
- AVENGERS EVERYBODY WANTS TO RULE THE WORLD

- AVENGERS INFINITY
- BLACK PANTHER WHO IS THE BLACK PANTHER?
- CAPTAIN AMERICA DARK DESIGNS
- CAPTAIN MARVEL LIBERATION RUN
- CIVIL WAR
- DEADPOOL PAWS
- SPIDER-MAN FOREVER YOUNG
- SPIDER-MAN KRAVEN'S LAST HUNT
- THANOS DEATH SENTENCE
- VENOM LETHAL PROTECTOR
- X-MEN DAYS OF FUTURE PAST
- X-MEN THE DARK PHOENIX SAGA
- SPIDER-MAN HOSTILE TAKEOVER

ART BOOKS
- *THE GUARDIANS OF THE GALAXY* THE ART OF THE GAME
- MARVEL'S AVENGERS: *BLACK PANTHER: WAR FOR WAKANDA* THE ART OF THE EXPANSION
- MARVEL'S *SPIDER-MAN MILES MORALES* THE ART OF THE GAME
- MARVEL'S *AVENGERS* THE ART OF THE GAME
- MARVEL'S *SPIDER-MAN* THE ART OF THE GAME
- MARVEL *CONTEST OF CHAMPIONS* THE ART OF THE BATTLEREALM
- *SPIDER-MAN: INTO THE SPIDER-VERSE* THE ART OF THE MOVIE
- THE ART OF IRON MAN THE ART OF THE MOVIE

STAR WARS LIBRARY

STAR WARS: THE MANDALORIAN GUIDE TO SEASON ONE

STAR WARS: THE MANDALORIAN GUIDE TO SEASON TWO

STAR WARS: THE EMPIRE STRIKES BACK: THE 40TH ANNIVERSARY SPECIAL EDITION

STAR WARS INSIDER: THE FICTION COLLECTION VOLUME 2

STAR WARS: THE SKYWALKER SAGA THE OFFICIAL COLLECTOR'S EDITION

STAR WARS: THE HIGH REPUBLIC: STARLIGHT STORIES VOLUME 1

- *ROGUE ONE: A STAR WARS STORY* THE OFFICIAL COLLECTOR'S EDITION
- *ROGUE ONE: A STAR WARS STORY* THE OFFICIAL MISSION DEBRIEF
- *STAR WARS: THE LAST JEDI* THE OFFICIAL COLLECTOR'S EDITION
- *STAR WARS: THE LAST JEDI* THE OFFICIAL MOVIE COMPANION
- *STAR WARS: THE LAST JEDI* THE ULTIMATE GUIDE
- *SOLO: A STAR WARS STORY* THE OFFICIAL COLLECTOR'S EDITION
- *SOLO: A STAR WARS STORY* THE ULTIMATE GUIDE
- THE BEST OF *STAR WARS INSIDER* VOLUME 1
- THE BEST OF *STAR WARS INSIDER* VOLUME 2

- THE BEST OF *STAR WARS INSIDER* VOLUME 3
- THE BEST OF *STAR WARS INSIDER* VOLUME 4
- *STAR WARS:* LORDS OF THE SITH
- *STAR WARS:* HEROES OF THE FORCE
- *STAR WARS:* ICONS OF THE GALAXY
- *STAR WARS:* THE SAGA BEGINS
- *STAR WARS* THE ORIGINAL TRILOGY
- *STAR WARS:* ROGUES, SCOUNDRELS AND BOUNTY HUNTERS
- *STAR WARS:* CREATURES, ALIENS, AND DROIDS
- *STAR WARS: THE RISE OF SKYWALKER* THE OFFICIAL COLLECTOR'S EDITION
- *STAR WARS: THE MANDALORIAN*: GUIDE TO SEASON ONE
- *STAR WARS: THE MANDALORIAN*: GUIDE TO SEASON TWO

- *STAR WARS: THE EMPIRE STRIKES BACK* THE 40TH ANNIVERSARY SPECIAL EDITION
- *STAR WARS: AGE OF RESISTANCE* THE OFFICIAL COLLECTORS' EDITION
- *STAR WARS: THE SKYWALKER SAGA* THE OFFICIAL COLLECTOR'S EDITION
- *STAR WARS INSIDER: FICTION COLLECTION* VOLUME 1
- *STAR WARS INSIDER PRESENTS: MANDALORIAN SEASON 2* VOLUME 1
- *STAR WARS INSIDER PRESENTS: MANDALORIAN SEASON 2* VOLUME 2
- *STAR WARS: THE HIGH REPUBLIC: STARLIGHT STORIES* VOLUME 1